SPECTRUM® READERS

LEVEL 2

HELPERS!
Dogs and People

RESCUE

By Teresa Domnauer

Carson-Dellosa Publishing

An imprint of Carson-Dellosa Publishing, LLC
P.O. Box 35665
Greensboro, NC 27425-5665

carsondellosa.com

Printed in the USA. All rights reserved.
ISBN 978-1-4838-0123-0

01-002141120

Dogs have different sizes, shapes, and abilities.

People love all kinds of dogs and rely on them to be helpers.

Dogs rely on people to help them, too. Look around, and you will see dogs and people helping each other.

Staying Safe

Dogs help people by guiding them to safety.

Specially trained dogs help people who are blind cross busy streets.

They help their owners ride buses and trains, too.

Guide dogs serve as "eyes" for people who cannot see.

Daily Living

Dogs help people who have special needs.

Service dogs are trained to assist in many important ways.

They open doors, pick up things that are dropped, and turn off lights.

They can even bark loudly to call for help if their owners need it.

Tracking

Dogs help people by tracking scents.
A dog's sense of smell is much more
sensitive than a person's.

Dogs learn smells quickly by sniffing
clothing or other items.

Then, they can track the scent to find
missing people and things.

Solving Crimes

Dogs help people by doing police work. Police dogs, known as K-9s, are specially trained.

They chase criminals, find missing people, and sniff out materials that could be dangerous.

Some police dogs have their own vests and badges!

Rescuing

Dogs help people by finding and rescuing those in danger.

Some rescue dogs work in cities.

Others, like this Saint Bernard, work high in the mountains.

They rescue skiers and hikers who are lost in the snow.

Hunting

Dogs help people when they hunt.
They can track scents through the woods.
They can swim in lakes to catch prey or chase it into trees.
Dogs fetch prey for hunters, too.

Herding

Dogs help people by herding animals.
On farms and ranches, dogs herd sheep
and cattle to keep them safe.
These working dogs are smart, nimble,
and very fast.
They race to herd up animals and
move them along for the farmers.

Getting Around

Dogs help people by pulling vehicles. Dogs like Alaskan huskies work in teams to pull sleds through the snow. Sled dogs are smart, fast, and powerful. Special scooters and wagons can be pulled by dogs, too.

Keeping Healthy

People help dogs by making sure they are healthy.

Good owners take their dogs to a veterinarian, or animal doctor.

Vets give shots to protect dogs from many diseases.

They check dogs for harmful fleas, ticks, and worms.

Grooming

People help dogs by keeping them clean.

Some owners bathe their dogs at home. Others hire groomers to scrub, brush, clip, and trim their pets.

Well-groomed dogs are happy and healthy.

Training

People help animals by teaching them. Dogs can be trained to listen to commands and perform jobs. Kindness and praise for good behavior help dogs learn. Dogs like knowing how to do useful jobs.

Competing

Dogs and people help each other at shows and competitions.

Dogs show off their amazing abilities to run, jump, and climb.

Owners enjoy spending time with their pets and winning awards.

The events are fun for animals and people.

Exercising

Dogs and people help each other exercise.

Dogs love to walk, run, and explore. People need to get up and move, too. Taking a walk is a great way for dogs and people to exercise.

Playing

Dogs and people help each other play. Running and playing catch together are good ways to exercise and have fun. People who spend time with their dogs have less stress.

Dogs like to spend time with people, too.

HELPERS! Dogs and People Comprehension Questions

1. Name three ways that dogs help people.

2. Name three ways that people help dogs.

3. How do service dogs help people with special needs?

4. What happens at dog shows and competitions?

5. Why is it important for dogs to see the vet regularly?

6. Why are dogs good at tracking scents?

7. Why is it important to clean and groom dogs?

8. What kinds of things can police dogs do?

9. What farm animals do dogs herd?

10. What are two ways people and dogs exercise and play together?